WILD AMERICA

CROW

By Lee Jacobs

BLACKBIRCH®
PRESS

THOMSON
★
GALE

San Diego • Detroit • New York • San Francisco • Cleveland • New Haven, Conn. • Waterville, Maine • London • Munich

THOMSON

━━━━━━━★━━━━━━━ ™

GALE

© 2003 by Blackbirch Press™. Blackbirch Press™ is an imprint of The Gale Group, Inc., a division of Thomson Learning, Inc.

Blackbirch Press™ and Thomson Learning™ are trademarks used herein under license.

For more information, contact
The Gale Group, Inc.
27500 Drake Rd.
Farmington Hills, MI 48331-3535
Or you can visit our Internet site at http://www.gale.com

Photo Credits: cover, pages 8, 14, 15 © Thomas Kitchin & Victoria Hurst, pages 3, 4, 5, 6, 7, 9, 10-11, 12, 16-17, 18-19, 22-23 © CORBIS; pages 20-21 © Digital Stock

LIBRARY OF CONGRESS CATALOGING-IN-PUBLICATION DATA

Jacobs, Lee.
  Crow / by Lee Jacobs.
    v. cm. — (Wild America)
Contents: The crow's environment — The crow body — Social life — The mating game
— Babies — Crows and humans.
  ISBN 1-56711-567-5 (hardback : alk. paper)
  1. Crows—Juvenile literature. [1. Crows.] I. Title. II. Series: Jacobs, Lee. Wild America.

QL696.P2367 J33 2003
598.8'64—dc21   2002013163

Printed in China
10 9 8 7 6 5 4 3 2 1

Contents

Introduction

Birds come in a huge number of colors and sizes, but they all have some things in common. All birds have wings and feathers. In fact, they are the only creatures on earth with feathers. Birds are warm-blooded. That means their body temperature stays about the same no matter what the outside environment is like. Birds hatch from eggs.

Crows are part of the Corvidae family, also called the crow family. This group includes jays, ravens, and magpies.

Crows live all over the world, except for Antarctica and South America. The American crow is the most common North American member of the crow family. It is found in many parts of the United States and Canada.

Top: Like all birds, crows hatch from eggs.
Bottom: Magpies are members of the crow family.

Other North American crows include the northwestern crow and the fish crow. The northwestern crow lives along the coast from Alaska to Oregon. The fish crow is seen near the coast all the way from New England to Texas.

A raven (pictured) is much larger than a crow. It has a wider wingspan, and its bill is thicker than a crow's.

Raven or Crow?

Crows and ravens look very much alike. In fact, people often confuse these close relatives. But there are ways to tell them apart. Ravens have wedge-shaped tails and thicker bills than crows. They are also more than twice the size of crows and have wider wingspans. And a raven's call sounds like "wonk-wonk," while a crow's call sounds like "caw-caw."

The Crow's Environment

Crows live in a wide range of habitats. They seem to like open fields as much as woodlands, and are seen along the coast as well as far inland. Crows are found in both crowded cities and rural towns. The only places crows do not seem to spend time are in deserts or on mountaintops.

The size of a crow family's territory depends on where it lives. In areas that have a lot of people, a crow's territory may take up about 10 acres (4 ha). In the country, a crow's area can be much larger. Crows will leave their territory and fly as far as 50 miles (80 km) away to search for food.

Crows may live in different habitats—including crowded coastal cities.

Most crows live in trees.

Crows usually live in trees. They do not build homes. During breeding season, they construct large, solid, but sloppy-looking nests within the home territory. Crows raise their young in these nests.

Many birds migrate, or travel to warmer places, for the winter. Most crows stay in their environment all year. But some migrate, especially those that live in colder northern climates. All crows (like other birds) can fluff up their feathers and trap a layer of warm air to protect them against the cold.

The Crow Body

American crows are large birds. They are usually about 17 to 21 inches (43 to 53 cm) long. They weigh 12 to 15 ounces (340 to 425 g). Northwestern and fish crows both look a lot like the American crow. They are slightly smaller, though—about 15 inches (38 cm) long. The span of the wings is normally about twice as long as the crow's body. Crows can fly at speeds between 25 and 30 miles (40 and 48 km) per hour.

A crow can fly at speeds up to 30 miles (48 km) per hour.

Male and female crows look the same. Crows have black beaks, legs, feet, and tails. Their feathers are also black, but they often have a glossy purplish sheen in the sunlight. Crow tails are fairly short and have a slightly squared shape. A crow has three front toes and a large hind toe on each of its narrow feet. All four toes have sharp, hooked claws. The hind toes help the crow grasp a branch tightly when it perches in a tree. Crows, like all birds, have no teeth. They use their powerful beaks to catch and hold food.

Crows have excellent hearing and eyesight, although they cannot see as well at night as they can during the day.

A crow has a sharp black beak. Its beak is powerful enough to catch and hold food.

Social Life

Crow families are often made up of a male and female and their offspring. Male crows are always dominant (in charge) over females. The young may include 3-year-old birds that have stayed with their parents, as well as babies. Sometimes two brothers live together, along with their female partners and all their offspring. This means family group sizes can vary.

Crows are very social creatures. Two crows will often help each other preen, or clean, hard-to-reach spots on their bodies, such as around the eyes and beak. When a group of crows feed together, one crow may sit high in a tree to act as a guard. It will warn the others of any danger that comes near. Crows will try to protect both members of their family and unrelated crows. They will also fiercely defend their territory, nests, and food.

Crows are social animals. They may help to clean each other and will protect each other even if they are not related.

The crow's main predators (animals that hunt other animals for food) are hawks and great horned owls. If attacked, crows will scream out alarm calls to each other. They gather in large numbers to scare off a predator or other threat.

The group will go after the enemy by pecking at it and cawing. Their loud calls can be heard at a great distance. Once the predator is driven away, the crows each go their own way. This violent response may be why a large group of crows is sometimes called a mob or a murder. (The scientific name for a group of crows is a flock.)

Crows use a variety of sounds to communicate. Scientists have studied more than 20 different crow calls. Many of these are used during breeding. Crows also send calls when they are hungry, ready to fight, or in distress. They can even mimic the sounds of humans and other animals. One way to tell the species of a crow is to listen to its song. Each type of crow has a slightly different call, although all of them reflect the "caw-caw" sound.

Crows are known to have more than 20 different calls.

During the day, crows usually travel alone or in small family groups. But on fall and winter nights, when it is not breeding season, crows often form huge flocks to sleep, or roost, in trees. One of these roosts might have anywhere from a few hundred birds to more than a million! These groups of crows usually meet about an hour before the sun goes down. The roosting area gets very noisy with their calls, and there is a constant flurry of activity. Once it is dark, the roost falls quiet. When the sun rises once again, both single birds and small groups fly off and go their own way for the day. Scientists are not sure exactly why crows come together in these huge roosts. It may help protect them from predators, since there can often be safety in numbers.

Bird Brains

Crows are very intelligent. Scientists think they are able to count and to tell a scarecrow from a real person. They can also solve problems. For example, crows know how to crack open shellfish by dropping them on rocks from high in the air. One scientist even proved that crows can remember a person who has invaded their nest. Adult crows saw the scientist climb trees to study young crows. Later, the adults chased him whenever he walked by—whether he was near the nests or not! Crows also seem to be able to tell the difference between a hunter armed with a gun and a farmer with a large tool. Crows may even use their own simple tools. A northwestern crow, for instance, used a stick to get a peanut that was stuck in a crack!

Hunters and Gatherers

Crows are omnivores, which means they eat both plant and animal food. To hunt for food on the ground, they look for movement and listen to sounds. They poke their strong beaks into holes, under stones, and into the ground to seek out tasty morsels. Crows eat small mammals and reptiles, insects, spiders, worms, snails, clams, and frogs. They dine on grains, fruits, seeds, and eggs of other bird species. Crows also eat carrion (dead animals). In fact, crows will eat just about anything. One reason these birds do well in areas where humans live is that crows will eat scraps they find in garbage cans and city dumps.

A crow finds a worm to eat. Crows can see and hear movement on the ground from high up in the air.

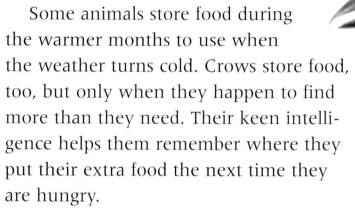

Some animals store food during the warmer months to use when the weather turns cold. Crows store food, too, but only when they happen to find more than they need. Their keen intelligence helps them remember where they put their extra food the next time they are hungry.

Because birds do not have teeth, much of their food is swallowed in larger pieces than it would be if it were chewed. The food in their stomachs often contains pieces of bone, fur, feathers, and other things that are hard to digest. To fix this problem, crows—like other birds—throw up tightly packed pellets that hold all the material their bodies cannot break down.

A crow does not chew its food. It swallows worms and other food in large pieces.

The Mating Game

The breeding season for crows begins in the early spring and can last until summer. Females are usually ready to breed at about 3 years of age. Males are not ready until they are about 5 years old. When a male finds a partner, he goes up to her and fluffs up his feathers. He then spreads his wings a bit and begins to bob up and down in a courtship dance. One or both of the crows may make sounds or try to preen the other's feathers. Once a crow finds a mate, they are paired for life.

Crows can be very territorial during mating season. A male and female build their nesting site together. They make a new nest each time they prepare to have babies, which is usually once a year. Crow nests are made out of large sticks and filled with mud and grass. They are big, bowl-shaped, and often very high off the ground—a crow's nest can be more than 100 feet (31 m) up a tree!

Female crows line their nests with soft materials, such as feathers, grass, and shredded bark.

The female crow also takes care to make sure the nest is cozy. She lines it with soft materials, such as feathers, shredded bark, grass, and fur. A female lays a clutch (group of eggs laid at one time) of 4 to 6 eggs. The eggs are olive green or blue green in color, with brownish speckles. The male gathers food and brings it to the female while she incubates the eggs. This means she sits on the eggs to keep them warm and help them develop. It takes 18 to 20 days for the eggs to hatch.

Babies

Baby crows are called nestlings. When they first hatch, they are completely helpless. They depend on their parents for survival. They have no feathers and cannot see. Their eyes open when they are about 5 days old. Within 10 days, they begin to get feathers. By about 4 weeks, they are fully feathered and ready to fly.

As the nestlings grow, the female helps the male find food for the family. She stays with the nestlings for 30 to 45 days, while they continue to develop. Both parents feed the nestlings, which mainly eat insects. American crows can be cooperative breeders. This means that several crows (usually older brothers and sisters) may help raise new babies.

Nestlings, or baby crows, stay with their mothers for up to 45 days after they hatch.

Young crows are in danger from predators. In fact, hawks, owls, raccoons, and even squirrels will eat both crow eggs and nestlings. The adult crows try to keep their young well hidden in the trees until they are larger. If a predator comes near, the parents may mob it and drive it away to keep their babies safe.

Many young crows stay with their families for a few years and help raise the next groups of nestlings. It is common for them to stay until they reach breeding age. At that time, the young crows leave to start their own families. They usually have many years in which to breed and raise families, since crows can live more than 10 years in the wild.

Owls and raccoons will eat crow eggs and nestlings.

Crows and Humans

Each year, humans kill millions of crows. They often target large roosts in order to get rid of many crows at once. Some people do not like crows because big flocks of them are loud and can ruin crops—especially corn. Others do not like them because crows sometimes eat the eggs of other birds. And some people think crows are scary because they have often been used as symbols of evil in books and movies.

Despite their bad reputation, crows help the environment in many ways. Crows help clean up roads when they eat carrion. They keep the insect population under control. Crows also cut down on the numbers of small rodents, such as mice and rats, that are seen as pests. Crows are smart, beautiful creatures that are not likely to become endangered despite human attempts to reduce their populations.

Crows are smart birds that can be satisfying animals to watch and interact with.

Glossary

carrion   dead or decaying animals

clutch   a group of eggs laid at one time

incubate   to develop and hatch eggs

nestling   a baby crow

omnivore   animals that eat plants and other animals

predator   an animal that hunts another animal for food

For Further Reading

Lerner, Carol. *Backyard Birds of Winter.* New York: Morrow Junior Books, 1994.

Markle, Sandra. *Outside and Inside Birds.* New York: Bradbury Press, 1994.

Pringle, Laurence. *Crows: Strange and Wonderful.* Honesdale, PA: Boyds Mills Press, 2002.

Index